Are You Thinking Like A Pharisee?

Growing In Grace

By

Dr. John L. Clinton Jr.

Are You Thinking Like a Pharisee?
By Dr. John L. Clinton Jr.

Published in the United States of America
by Tree of Life Publishing House, San Dimas, California

Library of Congress Control Number: 2008901156
Are You Thinking Like a Pharisee? / Dr. John L. Clinton Jr.
ISBN 978-0-9801357-4-9

Table of Contents

Acknowledgements

To God, My Heavenly Father, because He first loved me, He reached out to a sinner like me. And through His Son, I am afforded the gift of salvation, and the mind of Christ. To my faithful wife Dessa, I express a wide-open love for you which swallows up all there is about you. To my daughters Sherri and Rhonda, guess what? You two are the best! To my grandson Jonathan, who always reminds me, "I'm doing this just for you, Granddaddy."

Dedication

To the many who aspire to draw closer to God, but realize that a sinful nature can impede a Christian's spiritual growth. To those who discover that they have drifted and become subject to the sinful nature, but who continually submit themselves unto the Holy Spirit, in order to achieve moral discipline and the moral standards of the Law of God.

Introduction

A*re You Thinking Like a Pharisee?* This particular book was birthed out of my experiences with the Holy Spirit, whereas, God began to reveal to me that my attitude and actions towards others would ultimately determine how He would respond to me. The more of Himself that He reveals to me, the more God expects me to deal with others in a Christlike manner. There is much revelation that a believer must grasp, in order to aspire to higher levels of spiritual growth. However, the scriptures reveal the truth about God's word, and how we as Christians can progress from merely participating in religious activities to begin connecting with others outside of the church.

The modern day church is filled with a vast number of religious people, but how many of them are demonstrating a nature that depicts the mind of Christ? Many believers have adapted to the church's religious activities, but have neglected the principles that are relevant to God's word. In the Old Testament, there were two notable groups that had much to say about God and His word. These two groups were the Pharisees and the Sadducees. The Pharisees were diligent students and teachers of the Old Testament. The Sadducees were known as the powerful political leaders, which included the high priest and other leading officials of the Jerusalem Sanhedrin (composed of seventy people and a high priest).

The Pharisees believed strongly in maintaining the sacred character of the entire Old Testament and taught belief in the resurrection and judgment of the last day. The

Pharisees also believed in the existence of angels and spirits. On the other hand, the Sadducees denied the resurrection of Christ, nor did they believe in angels and spirits (Acts 23:6-8). Most often, it was the Pharisees who condemned Jesus Christ's teachings and emphasized the unimportant and neglected the weightier elements of the law, (Matthew 23:23-24).

The Pharisees added traditions to the law in order to make the law fit into the scheme of their own agenda, and their spiritual interpretation of it. The Pharisees reasoned among themselves that these traditions to the written law and interpretations of the law had been given by Moses to the Elders, and then had been transmitted orally down through the ages. Jesus referred to the Pharisees as being hypocrites on many occasions. The Pharisees were biblical scholars and wealthy with public status; therefore, they often had a tendency to despise those who did not agree with them. During Jesus' ministry, he was continually challenged by the Pharisees regarding the interpretation of the scriptures.

By now, you probably have drawn a conclusion about the attitude and conduct displayed by the Pharisees. At this point, I want to ask you a few questions: Have you ever became so stubborn that despite hearing the truth, you forged forward and failed to act upon that truth? Are you learning the scriptures merely to be capable of quoting and impressing others, or are you allowing God to speak to you through His word? The Pharisees could quote scriptures, but the truth about God's word was not apparent in their lives. God does not want Christians to think like the Pharisees. Instead, God wants you and me to develop spiritually with the mind of Christ.

In Ephesians 4:22-24, Paul teaches that
"You were taught, with regard to your former way of

life, to put off your old self, which is being corrupted by its deceitful desires; to be made new in the attitude of your mind; and to put on the new self, created to be like God in true righteousness and holiness."

One thing is for certain-- when a Christian seeks the guidance of the Holy Spirit, whether it deals with conflict, marriage, relationships, job, or any other needs that warrants spiritual discernment, the Holy Spirit will always begin to show the things that need to be changed about yourself. Why does the Holy Spirit begin to show seekers their flaws first? God knows that attitudes and beliefs must change in us first, before we can effectively affect change in others. For example, take the father that prays for a change to occur regarding his family, even when his deeds and actions are less than desirable as the head of his household. God will respond to his prayer through him, and the father must be willing to submit and follow the counsel of the Holy Spirit. Look at the employee who always says, "I don't have a problem, they're the ones you should be questioning." However, this particular employee is always expressing his or her concerns about an unfriendly work environment. God wants to change us first. As Christians, whether it's the home or the workplace, God wants the Holy Spirit to begin working in us. Then we will no longer allow the environment to change us; rather, we will become agents for change in any environment.

In this book, I share with you principles that I have employed throughout the years; they have been proven efficient to guide and empower. Moreover, the principles you will learn will enable you to face challenges as Jesus did. Together, we will study the legacy of the Pharisees, and see what we can learn about their attitudes, behaviors, and beliefs that Jesus described when He said, "I called these types of people hypocrites."

Section One

God's Moral Law Police

Are You an Expert Concerning God's Moral Laws?

It is without a doubt that Jesus was the greatest teacher who ever taught on earth. Even today, Jesus' teachings surpass all of humankind's intelligence. Therefore, the Holy Spirit is essential in the discernment of God's word. However, during the onset of Jesus' ministry, the Holy Spirit had not been sent by Jesus to reside within the hearts and minds of those who believed and put their faith and trust in God. Therefore, a bewildering question may exist within some believers' minds. Could the Pharisees possibly understand Jesus teachings without the help of the Holy Spirit?

I believe the answer to that question is an overwhelming

yes. God has always communicated to His people, and answered their calls, whether through prophets, priests, and yes, even through a donkey (Numbers 22:28-30). The Pharisees were experts on the Law of God, but can a believer live and develop the moral discipline required to meet the demands of God's moral standards? Can he or she achieve righteousness without the help of the Holy Spirit? In Isaiah 6: 6, God likened mankind's righteousness to filthy rags. Scripture highlights human iniquities (we all fade as a leaf in the wind), and therefore, it is through God's righteousness that believers are made righteous.

The Pharisees were essentially being the sheriff and judge within the same court room. But in the end, there will only be one judge--God is in control of everything here on earth and in heaven. The tragedy is that most believers fail to listen to the voice of God. We must trust/obey God's word and believe what the scriptures reveal about God, or reject the Gospel of Jesus Christ. As believers we must realize that there is no middle ground: you either enter into the Kingdom of God or the Kingdom of Darkness. Jesus said in Matthew 5:20,

> *"For I tell you that unless your righteousness surpasses that of the Pharisees and the teachers of the law, you will certainly not enter the Kingdom of heaven."*

The Pharisees were great at adding rules and regulations to the original Law of Moses, while doing nothing to help others keep them. Moreover, the Pharisees often invented ways to omit them altogether in their own lives.

The Pharisees' main agenda was to appear outwardly as followers and keepers of the law, but inwardly they rejected Jesus and His teachings. The attitudes of the Pharisees may seem familiar at times, but what about yours and mine? In that, we often discover that our thoughts and actions towards others do not depict the spirit of the law.

For example, have you ever found yourself in opposition to the teachings of Christ because you were wronged by someone? Moreover, how did you handle your situation? God's word indicates that we should forgive each other for our trespasses. The Pharisees were often arrogant towards other Jews as well, and therefore, were widely known as being hypocrites because they were attempting to live above God's law.

I think it's safe to say that the Pharisees were self-righteous and self-centered. Moreover, they focused on their own agenda, other than the dispensation of the wisdom and knowledge of God. Jesus said that these types of people were not following the spirit of the law. Jesus was focus on the spirit of the law (the way in which we reach out and meet the spiritual and physical needs of each other). It is one thing to talk about meeting a need, but results only manifest in the doing. Are you thinking like a Pharisee? Are you making yourself available for His service? Are you just too busy to serve? Below are a few wisdom keys that can help you stay Christ-centered:

1. Pray.
2. Listen to the voice of God.
3. Do things for God's greater glory.
4. Do things without complaining and disputing that you are blameless, harmless, or without fault in the midst of a crooked and perverse world.
5. Shine as a light in the world; allow people to see Jesus in you.
6. Hold fast to the word of life (read God's word).
7. Bless those who persecute you (Romans 12:14).
8. Do not repay evil with evil (Romans 12:17).
9. Love your enemies (Matthew 5:44).
10. Pray for those who persecute you (Matthew 5:44).

I must concede that God's word can often seem strange; however, I have found that,

"*As for God, his way is perfect; the word of the Lord is flawless. He is a shield for all who take refuge in him.*"
2 Samuel 2:31

A believer's thoughts, actions, and deeds should not be contrary to Jesus' teachings. Instead, Christians should be rising up to the level of righteousness that Christ has to offer, and not accepting the world's substitute (sin). God desires that His believers be clothed in His righteousness. God sent his son to ensure the law was fulfilled (the wages of sin is death). Because of God's grace and mercy, a sinner is given an invitation to salvation.

Christians are challenged with grasping the spirit of the law, not just the moral standards of it. As Christians we should never give service to others with the intent of achieving some sort of personal gain or recognition, but allow others to see the true spirit in giving (Jesus Christ). In Matthew 6:3-4, Jesus said, that the Father sees you when you give and will reward you. Are you thinking like a Pharisee? Guess what? God wants you to start thinking again.

The Good News

Do you tell people about the good news (the gospel of Jesus Christ)? Everyone who believes in Jesus Christ is offered a free gift from God-- "salvation." Have you learned to put your total trust and faith in God? The Pharisees professed their beliefs outwardly, but secretly they rejected Jesus' teaching. During one of Jesus' appearances after His resurrection, Jesus told his disciples,

"Go into all the world and preach the good news to all creation. Whoever believes and is baptized will be saved, but whoever does not believe will be condemned."
Mark 16:15

I have an ongoing story to tell you that happens to me often in my profession. However, before I tell you my story, let's observe John 3:12, which depicts a man named Nicodemus who visited Jesus at night.

"Now there was a man of the Pharisees named Nicodemus, a member of the Jewish ruling council. He came to Jesus at night and said, Rabbi, we know you are a teacher who has come from God. For no one could perform the miraculous signs you are doing if God were not with him." John 3:12

The odd thing about Nicodemus is that he visited Jesus at night, seemingly to avoid any contact with Jesus doing the day. Did Nicodemus want to avoid the crowds that often were around Jesus? Did Nicodemus fear opposition from other religious leaders? Often, people who do evil hate the light and prefer the darkness for fear that their deeds will be exposed. We can certainly surmise that Nicodemus's visited Jesus at night, because he had a hidden agenda. I teach high school, and there is an ongoing battle concerning issues that relate to the separation of church and state. I am often reminded of the approach Nicodemus used to ask Jesus a few questions. He came to Jesus at night.

A great number of teachers at my school often ask me questions about religious matters or activities. I enjoy teaching about the Gospel of Jesus Christ, but the interesting thing is that in most cases, they come to me when I am alone. First, I will tell you that I do not teach Christ in the classroom. I was hired to teach certain subjects, and I honor God by doing the work that I was contracted to do. You maybe thinking that the reason I don't teach Christ to my students, is because I am afraid of the school's administration. I can assure you, I am not afraid of the administration department. I am fortunate to be teaching within one of the finest school districts within the city of San Antonio, Texas.

"I don't teach Christ; I live Christ." Therefore, it is through the demonstration of Jesus' teachings that I have led many people to Him. What about you? Are you teaching Christ? Are you demonstrating His teachings? Remember! The only Bible some people may ever read will probably be your life. The Pharisees taught God's law to His people, but they were not demonstrating the moral character defined within the law. God wants a believer to represent Him in meaningful ways to others, especially through their deeds and actions towards one another. God desires that you and I become His light to others, which will ultimately lead to winning souls.

I believe what distinguishes some Christians from others is a true conviction of their faith and trust in God. Are you ashamed of the Gospel of Jesus Christ? Do you allow people to see Jesus in you; or are they merely looking at you? To find out if you are thinking like a Pharisee, you only have to ask yourself the following questions:

1. Do you put others ahead of your own agenda?

2. Can people see Jesus through your deeds and actions?

3. Are you helping others succeed in life?

Jesus was effective not only because he was a great teacher; Jesus also was a great demonstrator of his teachings. Jesus commanded His disciples to go throughout the nations and tell others about the good news, but live their lives and touch others according to the dispensation of the gospel. Jesus demonstrated God's love in the dispensation of His gospel. I continue to love and answer the questions some teachers propose to me, even though some secretly meet with me. I read an interesting quote one day, which said, "People don't care how much you know, until they know you care." How true! Jesus touched the hearts of the people because he cared. Below are some interesting facts that I have discovered about God and people.

- Know God at the level that enables Him to work through your life.
- A Christian should not hide facts about his or her life (everyone has been through something).
- Show evidence of your triumphing and spiritual growth.
- God chose you to become a witness for His greater glory.
- A Christian can communicate to others the message of the cross and the difference God has made his or her life.
- People often read the lives of others. Some people will probably never read the Bible, but they will definitely read your life.

God will give a believer a testimony, a communication that links others with your past, and allow people to see God's work in you. The Pharisees were attempting to hide the truth about God's word. However, God has given you and me the grace to do the work, and through your efforts, others will realize their restoration, healing, and deliverance. You are concerned about the well-being and spiritual growth of others, aren't you? To think like a Pharisee is to think only of yourself.

Jesus Touched Sinful
People Too!

How comfortable are you in the midst of sinful people, especially those that have not accepted or maybe don't understand the Gospel? Jesus did not allow sinful acts committed by people to stop the dispensation of His gospel. In Luke 7:36-39, Jesus was invited to eat at a Pharisee's home.

"Now one of the Pharisees invited Jesus to have dinner with him, so he went to the Pharisee's house and reclined at the table. When a woman who had lived a sinful life in that town learned that Jesus was eating at the Pharisee's house, she brought an alabaster jar of perfume, and as she stood behind him at his feet weeping, she begin to wet his feet with her tears. Then she wiped them with her hair, kissed them and poured perfume on them. When the Pharisee who had invited him saw this, he said to himself, if this man were a prophet, he would know who is touching him and what kind of woman she is –that she is a sinner."

Jesus not only taught in the synagogues, he also demonstrated his teachings in the streets wherever he went. I am often grieved by the attitudes and beliefs of many of God's people, whereas, we dress up on Sunday mornings and attend church services but seldom take the gospel into the streets. Many of God's servants are uncomfortable with reaching people that are caught up in societal systems such as prisons, shelters, nursing homes, orphanages, and half-way homes.

During one of Jesus' visits to the synagogue, the scroll of the prophet Isaiah was handed to him. Jesus unrolled the scroll and began reading,

"The Spirit of the Lord is on me, because he has anointed me to preach good news to the poor. He has sent me to proclaim freedom for the prisoners and recovery of sight for the blind, and release the oppressed, to proclaim the year of the Lord's favor."

What do you do that relates to the good news Jesus proclaimed (sight for the blind, release of the oppressed, good news to the poor)? How do you serve in ways that allow people to see Jesus working through you? Jesus also cautions Christians when carrying out the mandates of the gospel, whether it's through giving, good deeds, or prayer, to be careful not to become self-righteous when you do so (do not think too highly of yourself). For example, in Matthew 6:1-4, Jesus said,

"Be careful not to do your acts of righteous before men, to be seen by them. If you do, you will have no reward from your Father in heaven. So when you give to the needy, do not announce it with trumpets, as the hypocrites do in the synagogues and on the streets, to be honored by men. But when you give to the needy, do not let your left hand know what your right hand is doing, so that your giving may be in secret. Then your Father, who sees what is secret, will reward you."

Likewise, Jesus said in Matthew 6:5-8,

"And when you pray, do not be like the hypocrites for they love to pray standing in the synagogues and on the street corners to be seen by men. But when you pray, go into your room, close the door and pray to your Father, who is unseen. Then your Father, who sees what is done in secret, will reward you. And when you pray, do not keep on babbling like pagans, for they think they will

be heard because of their many words. Do not be like them, for your Father knows what you need, before you ask him."

Jesus commissioned his disciples in Matthew 28:19 to go and make disciples of all nations, baptizing them in the name of the Father and the Son and the Holy Spirit and to teach obedience to everything He had commanded. Therefore, believers must touch the lives of the unsaved and sinful as well as the homeless, the drug addict, the sick, and, yes, the prostitute, too. Most of the people I have mentioned probably will not be attending Sunday morning church services; however, you will find them in the streets. God loves these people, too! The Pharisees thought little about the kinds of people that Jesus touched because many were denounced guilty by the law. However, Jesus came to fulfill the requirements of the law and not to abolish it; therefore, those that had failed to maintain the moral standards depicted in the law were capable of a moral achievement through their faith and trust in Jesus Christ. God wants you and me to give His message of grace and mercy to others, and through repentance He will allow a believer to begin again. God's law was given to Moses to govern the moral conduct of each of our lives, and Jesus sent the Holy Spirit to help in the moral achievement of it.

The Pharisees often passed their judgments towards other people. Do you sometime judge people according to your own standards? Jesus cautioned about judging people,

"Do not judge, or you too will be judged. For the same way you judge others, you will be judged, and with the same measure you use, it will be measured to you" Matthew 7:1-2.

Jesus is the judge of mankind. I must confess that I have in the past been critical of others. Today, I listen to the Holy

Spirit when my thoughts are contrary to Jesus' teachings. I put on the mind of Christ. To be critical of others is to think and act like the Pharisees did; however, to put on the mind of Christ is to love others regardless of offenses and trespasses.

God hates sin but still loves His people. As Christians we don't have to allow a sinful environment to change us; we can change the environment. Jesus did. You may be saying, "I am not Jesus," and you are absolutely correct. However, you do have the Holy Spirit working in you. Here is a final thought: If you lead one person to Christ, guess what? God will reward you. However, if you think like a Pharisee you will not lead anyone to Christ. Christians that allow the Holy Spirit to guide their daily thoughts, actions, and deeds toward others are thinking with the mind of Christ.

A Pharisee Will Always Attempt to Distort the Truth of God's Word

Without a doubt, the Pharisees were the group who could have given God's people a greater revelation of scripture. Nonetheless, they chose to distort God's word through faulty interpretations of it. The Pharisees kept God's people ignorant and confused regarding God's law and His plan for salvation. Jesus warns the Pharisees in Luke 11:52 about distorting the truth of God's word and the consequences of their actions:

"Woe to you experts in the law, because you have taken away the key to knowledge. You yourselves have not entered, and you have hindered those who were entering."

I believe it is better to have not known God's law at all, than to receive a misguided interpretation of it.

Jesus tells believers in Luke 12:1

"be on guard against the yeast of the Pharisees, which is hypocrisy."

Jesus used the word yeast as being symbolic of evil or corruption. The idea is that a small amount of yeast is capable of fermenting a large amount of dough. Therefore, a believer cannot allow his or herself to foster the mindsets, attitudes, or behaviors that are clearly secular. So how do Christians guard against the things that Jesus often denounced, especially avoiding the ideals, attitudes, and behaviors that the Pharisees exhibited? Below are some keys which I constantly employ in order to avoid the ways of the Pharisees.

- Pray
- Seek the counsel of the Holy Spirit
- Listen to the voice of God
- Read God's word, for the Bible reveals the truth about creation, the world, and the hereafter
- Do not be passive in situations; a passive will gives in to temptation.
- Control your thought life; perverted thoughts will always lead to sin.

The keys that I have outlined above have helped me and can help you also walk in the wisdom of God. A good place to start teaching yourself wisdom keys is within the book of Proverbs. The book of Proverbs reveals wisdom keys that can help you avoid undesirable people and various situations that can bring hardships into your life. Proverbs are God's instructions concerning our actions and the possible consequences of them. Finally, you may be thinking, well, I don't give a faulty interpretation of the scriptures to others. God has commanded that as Christians we read and learn about His word, and we cannot carry out the Gospel unless we know it.

Remember! Some people have yet to grasp the importance of reading God's word, and therefore, the message which they interpret through your deeds and actions may be accepted as the gospel truth. It isn't good enough to know about the gospel of Jesus Christ; we must be capable of explaining the gospel to others. Now, isn't that the gospel truth!

What is the Law of God?

By now, I'm sure you have come to realize that the religious leaders and high officials were the main trespassers of the Law of God. These groups came under constant condemnation by Jesus because their deeds and behavior were in total opposition of Jesus' teachings. They emphasized the unimportant and neglected the weightier elements of the law (Matthew 23:23-24). The Pharisees added traditions to the law in order to make the law fit into their scheme of spiritually and scripture discernment. Jesus continually revealed errors in their faulty discernment of the law. The Bible Dictionary defines the law as a term applied in the New Testament to the Mosaic legislation, and sometimes to the whole dispensation as distinguished from the dispensation under the Gospel, The Bible Dictionary (Jubilee Publishers).

Now that we have established what is the Law of God, let's explore a bit further to surmise how the Pharisees were faulty in their judgment and discernment of the law. Paul reveals in Romans 4:14-15,

"For if those who live by law are heirs, faith has no value
and the promise is worthless, because law brings wrath.
And where there is no law there is no transgression."

Paul explains that the law points to sin when clearly defined boundaries have been overstepped. Also, the law reveals transgressions, but not the promise of God (see Romans 4:13).

Paul further exhorts in Romans 5:20:21,

*"The law was added so that the trespass might increase.
But where sin increased, grace increased all the more,
so that, just as sin reigned in death, so also grace might
reign through righteousness to bring eternal life through
Jesus Christ our Lord."*
Paul tells believers in Romans 6:14,
*"For sin shall not be your master, because you are not
under law, but under grace."*

In the scriptures outlined above, Paul is not suggesting that Christians live free from all moral authority. Paul realized that sin enslaved God's people. Being under the law in the Old Testament era did nothing to empower God's people to resist sin. However, Paul believed that grace empowered the Body of Christ. What did Paul realize about God's grace that the Pharisees overlooked?

In Titus 2:11-14 grace is explained,
*"For the grace of God that brings salvation has appeared
to all men. It teaches us to say no to ungodliness and
worldly passions, and to live self-controlled, upright
and godly lives in this present age, while we wait for the
blessed hope-the glorious appearing of our great God and
Savior, Jesus Christ, who gave himself for us to redeem
us from all wickedness and to purify for himself a people
that are his very own, eager to do what is good."*

God showed His undeserved and unmerited love while we were still sinners. The idea that works or religious acts can some how buy entrance into God's kingdom is nonsense. Believers are saved by their faith in Jesus Christ, and therefore, God grants grace to enter His kingdom. God's grace rescues believers from their guilt, judgment, and condemnation, and prepares the believer for good works. You may have been bound by the law, however; believers have been released from the law in order that we may serve in the new way of the Spirit, and not the old way of the

written code (Romans 7:6).

God's law is still vital for believers, because it serves as a moral and ethical guide for believers. Christians obey the law out of love for God, and by the power of the Holy Spirit. The Pharisees and other religious leaders, even with all of their intelligence amassed, never really understood Jesus' teachings. Jesus had been sent for their benefit, too:

> *"For what the law was powerless to do in that it was weakened by the sinful nature, God did by sending his own Son in the likeness of sinful man to be a sin offering. And so he condemned sin in sinful man, in order that the righteous requirement of the law might be fully met in us, who do not live according to the sinful nature but according to the Spirit."* Romans 8:3-4

Jesus freed believers from the condemnation, judgment, and guilt that follow the trespass of God's law. Jesus perfectly fulfilled the demands of the law; however, the law is still an important part of God's written code. The Holy Spirit will help believers meet its moral demands. Christ is the end of the law.

> *"Christ is the end of the law, so that there may be righteousness for everyone who believes."*
> Romans 10:4

Section Two

The Work of the Holy Spirit

God Responded to the Pharisee's Misguided Interpretations of His law with a New Testament Solution

The Holy Spirit

I would like to shift the theme of our discussion from the Pharisees and talk about the work of the Holy Spirit. The Spirit of God can help a believer avoid thinking like a Pharisee. First, let's review a new covenant that God talks about in Hebrews 10:11-18:

"Day after day every priest stands and performs his religious duties; again and again he offers the same

sacrifices, which can never take away sin. But when this priest had offered for all time one sacrifice for sin, he sat down at the right hand of God. Since that time he waits for his enemies to be made his footstool, because by one sacrifices he has made perfect forever those who are being made holy."

The Holy Spirit also testifies to us about this:

"This is the covenant I will make with them after that time, says the Lord. I will put my laws in their hearts, and I will write them in their minds. Then he adds; their sins and lawless acts I will remember no more."

Halleluiah! God has revealed in scripture the measure of His grace, which transcends the Law of Moses. Paul tells the Corinthians in 1:14-16 that

"The man without the spirit does not accept the things that come from the Spirit of God, for they are foolishness to him, and he cannot understand them, because they are spiritual discerned. The spiritual man makes judgment about all things, but he himself is not subject to any man's judgment: for who has known the mind of the Lord that he may instruct him? But we have the mind of Christ."

Paul is telling the Corinthians that the unbeliever follows his or her natural instincts, whereas this passion is ruled by a worldly perspective on life. He or she does not possess the Holy Spirit, and therefore, cannot receive from the Spirit of God. Paul also reminded the Corinthians that all people are law breakers, whereby we stand guilty and condemned to death. However, it is the Spirit of the living God which gives life and the promise of a new covenant (2 Corinthians 3:6). In order to avoid thinking like a Pharisee, Christians must learn to live by the Spirit and not gratify the desires of the sinful nature. The sinful nature and the Spirit are in conflict with each other; the Spirit wars against the sinful nature. Christians that are led by the Spirit are not under the law, (Galatians 5:16-18).

By now, you should be developing an understanding of why the Pharisees failed to grasp Jesus' message concerning the spirit in which the dispensation of the law is given to God's people. The Pharisees rejected Jesus message concerning God's new covenant and chose to remain bound by the law. The Pharisees continued to act out of their sinful nature (hatred, discord, selfish ambition, dissension, rage, jealousy, to name a few-- for a detail listing of the sinful nature read Galatians 5:19-21). The Apostle Paul warns that people that live this way will not inherit the Kingdom of God. A believer's character is produced by the Holy Spirit.

In order to guard against the sinful nature, which is present in every human being, we must cooperate with the Holy Spirit. The Holy Spirit produces such fruits as (love, joy, peace, patience, kindness, goodness, faithfulness, gentleness and self control (Galatians 5:22-23). Paul also exalts that against these types of fruits there is no law. The Holy Spirit will guide believers through life, and help them discern truth concerning all circumstances or situations. Jesus told His disciples that he would send a helper to guide them in all truth; that helper still exists today and is known as the Holy Spirit. Why not allow the Holy Spirit to become your guide in life? After all, the Holy Spirit speaks in God's authority.

Below are some scripture references that will give you a better understanding of the work of the Holy Spirit.

- John 15:26 (Holy Spirit testifies)
- John 16:8 (Holy Spirit convicts of sin)
- John 16:13 (Holy Spirit guides)
- Acts 2:1-4 (The Coming of the Holy Spirit)
- Acts 13:2 (Holy Spirit speaks to believers)
- Romans 6:11 (we must die to sin and come alive in

Christ)
- Romans 8:14 (Holy Spirit leads)
- Romans 8:26 (Holy Spirit is an intercessor)
- Romans 12:2 (sin no longer has control over your life)
- 1 Corinthians 6:19-20 (surrender ourselves unto the Holy Spirit)

"When the day of Pentecost came, they were all together in one place. Suddenly a sound like a blowing of a violent wind came from heaven and filled the whole house where they were sitting. They saw what seemed to be tongues of fire that separated and came to rest on each of them. All of them were filled with the Holy Spirit and began to speak in other tongues as the Spirit enabled them" (Acts 2:1-4).

Note: The Day of Pentecost is recorded in the Bible as being the first fruits of Christ's church and the beginning of a great harvest of souls. Those who believed in the gospel of Jesus Christ were joined through the work of the Holy Spirit.

How are your "Beatitudes?

I believe that a Christian's attitude will determine his or her altitude in Christ. The more a believer aspires to learn and live according to Christ's teachings, the more of Himself He will reveal, which will ultimately lead to living a godly and Spirit filled life. On one occasion, Jesus was traveling through Galilee teaching in synagogues, and preaching about the good news of the kingdom. People began to bring their diseased and sick to him. Jesus healed them all, the demon-possessed, those with seizures, the paralyzed, those suffering severe pain, and those ill with various disease, (Matthew 4:23-25).

The people began to follow Jesus, and large crowds from Galilee, Decapolis, Jerusalem, Judea, and the region across the Jordan followed him. Jesus used this opportunity to teach one of the most important messages while He was here on earth. What was Jesus' message to the people? You can really summarize Jesus' message with only one word, "Attitude." Jesus went up on a mountainside, sat down surrounded by His disciples, and began to teach them:

"Blessed are the poor in spirit, for theirs is the kingdom of heaven. Blessed are those who mourn, for they will be comforted. Blessed are the meek, for they will inherit the earth. Blessed are those who hunger and thirst for righteousness, for they will be filled. Blessed are the merciful, for they will be shown mercy. Blessed are the pure in heart, for they will see God. Blessed are the peacemakers, for they will be called sons of God. Blessed

are those who are persecuted because of righteousness, for theirs is the kingdom of heaven. Blessed are you when people insult you, persecute you and falsely say all kinds of evil against you because of me. Rejoice and be glad, for in the same way they persecuted the prophets who were before you."

Jesus message was filled with godly attributes and principles that are important to Christians, if we are to become effective ministers of the Gospel. The meek, the merciful, the poor in heart, and peacemakers are characteristic members of God's kingdom. How often do you show mercy to others? God searches the hearts of humankind, whereas man looks at the outer appearance. Christians cannot afford to allow ungodly thoughts to enter their minds, thoughts which will eventually pollute their hearts (conviction takes place in a believer's heart, and a believer's mind will produce the seed of his or her thoughts).

It is also impossible to become a follower of Jesus Christ, (without becoming a peacemaker, Jesus is the Prince of Peace.) God will bless you for displaying a godly attitude towards others. You will enter the Kingdom of God with these qualities. In the Beatitudes, Jesus taught the people God's discourse on the law and His principles. In His message to them, Jesus also captured God's blessings and praises for living a godly life.

There is a contrast between the outward demand of the law and the inner attitude, which God desires. Below is the contrast depicted in scripture.

Law	**Spirit**
(It was said)	(But I tell you)
Do not *Murder*	Do not *Anger*
Do not commit *Adultery*	Do not *Lust*
Do not *Divorce*	Stay *Committed*

Do not break an *Oath*	Do not *Swear* at all
Do not return *Evil* for evil	*Forgive*
Love your *Neighbor* and Hate your *Enemy*	Love Your *Enemy*

Note: See Matthew 5:21-48 for contrast of the Law and Gospel. After Jesus finish teaching these Beatitudes, he emphasized to the people that a person's deeds should follow their words. Jesus told them:

"You are the salt of the earth. But if the salt loses its saltiness, how can it be made salty again? It is no longer good for anything, except to be thrown out and trampled by men. You are the light of the world. A city on a hill cannot be hidden. Neither do people light a lamp and put it under a bowl. Instead they put it on its stand, and it gives light to everyone in the house. In the same way, let your light shine before men, that they may see your good deeds and praise your Father in heaven" (Matthew 5:13-16).

How are your Beatitudes? A believer's attitude is made known in his or her words and actions towards others. Is your light shining bright for Christ, so that others can see and come to know Him? Or is your attitude hiding your light under a bowl? Why not put your light on the stand so that everyone that enters God's house can see? You are the salt of the earth. *"When you adjust your beatitudes towards people, God will change their attitude towards you."*

Will you pray this prayer with me?

PRAYER:
Father I submit myself totally unto the Holy Spirit, that you might lead me in the discourse of the Gospel of Jesus Christ, so that others

might see your light shining bright in me. I pray that my actions will follow my words, and that all I do will be in Jesus' name, and not my own. I will display a good attitude regardless of the circumstances or situations that may engulf my life. I will learn to be kind to those that persecute or show hatred toward me. I will obey the law which you have given to your people and allow the Holy Spirit to guide me in achieving its moral standards. Amen.

Am I righteous enough to serve Christ?

Often Christians are given positions of authority within the church's organizational structure; some may serve as greeters, ushers, deacons, elders, associate ministers, on committees, or as leaders of a bible study. Even though human beings are inherently flawed, it is the manner in which these particular spiritual/administrative duties are employed that pleases God. I struggle with what I am about to discuss with you, but it needs to be said. I have witnessed this particular scenario played out often in churches, whereas, the abuse of power is exhibited. Because of God's grace and mercy, believers are afforded the opportunity to grow spiritually and economically in the church. However, over time I have seen many of selected leaders begin to think and act like the Pharisees.

Some leaders begin to think that they have an entire revelation of the Bible. Others might exhibit attitudes of righteousness, even more than the Messiah. Some leaders may even begin to form clicks or polarized groups. I believe these types of public display of attitude send the wrong messages throughout the congregation, especially to new converts. I have seen new converts leave the church altogether because of an unfriendly or seemingly uncaring attitude of the church leadership. Moreover, mature believers will often leave as well, because of jealousy, strife, and the selfish attitudes of some of the church leaders. People have various reasons for attending church service;

however, I am more than certain that hidden deep within the hearts of God's people there is a need to get to know their God, and a greater revelation of His word. However, in most cases the church holds a grim reminder of the behaviors and actions exhibited by the Pharisee. Therefore, the unbeliever and the new convert retreat back into the shadows of darkness, thinking to themselves, is this really what the church is all about? What is spiritual leadership all about? In simple terms, spiritual leadership is all about God, and zero about ourselves. Spiritual leadership focuses on God's agenda, not our own. Moreover, people get to see Christ working through the believer. Christ always made a distinction between Himself and the Father. People often look for God when they are suffering, hurting, or seeking some sort of blessing beyond their capability. Many come to church to find God in their circumstance or situation, or to reclaim what was stolen or lost along their journey in life.

As Christians we should not look down on these kinds of people, the prostitute, the thief, the prisoner, the divorcee, the teenage mother, and yes the murderer, too. I have personally ministered to these kinds of people while serving in the church's outreach programs. These people need to hear about the Gospel of Jesus Christ and that their deeds have not placed them beyond His saving grace. God's grace and mercy is limitless; He has enough for everyone. Jesus encountered a person during His ministry:

> *"The teachers of the law and the Pharisees brought in a woman caught in adultery. They made her stand before a group and said to Jesus, Teacher; this woman was caught in the act of adultery.   In the Law Moses commanded us to stone such women. Now what do you say? They were using this question as a trap; in order to have a basis for accusing him. But Jesus bent down and*

started to write on the ground with his finger. When they kept on questioning him, he straightened up and said to them. If any one of you is without sin let him be the first to throw a stone at her." John 8:3-8

Jesus did not let sin become an obstacle between him and a person's soul. Most often, it is the ones that society holds condemned to the highest degree, who become the most effective witnesses for the glory of God. Are you righteous enough to serve God? To tell the truth, none of us are! It is through a believer's faith in Jesus Christ that a believer is made righteous (see Romans 3:21-24). King Solomon, the richest and wisest man biblical history records that ever lived, shares some helpful instructions on the subject of righteousness in Ecclesiastes 7:15-16:

"In this meaningless life of mine I have seen both of these: a righteous man perishing in his righteousness, and a wicked man living long in his wickedness. Do not be over-righteous, neither be over-wise –why destroy yourself."

The Pharisees saw themselves as being righteous before God. However, scripture reveals that they did nothing to help the people understand and obey God's laws. The Pharisees only added more rules and regulations to God's law, in order to satisfy their selfish desires. As a church leader, what example or message are you communicating at your church? Are you demonstrating Jesus' teachings to others? How do you react when you are asked to serve in unfamiliar areas of your church? Do leaders argue among themselves? Do you show the proper respect for spiritual authority? Maybe you have become Mr. or Mrs. Righteousness, in that your character has surpassed the moral, upright, and blameless standards of God's law.

I salute those that have achieved the moral discipline that is necessary for moral achievement, in the Law of

God. Therefore, God's grace and mercy is unnecessary for you. As for me, I am so thankful for the dispensation of the Gospel of Jesus Christ, whereas, His grace rescues me more often than I would like to admit. I am also thankful for His mercies being made fresh each dawning of a new day. God's love for His people is so powerful; without the love of God working within me, I would be left with the idea of eradicating myself, what a scary thought! Solomon gives further insight into his thoughts on righteousness,

> *"There is not a righteous man on earth who does what is right and never sins."* Ecclesiastes 7:20

Are you righteous enough to serve God? Let me pose the question another way; Do you make your self-available for His service and serve in the manner that Jesus demonstrated to the Pharisees? Jesus served others with love, compassion, grace and mercy; Jesus demonstrated His teachings while He was here on earth. Isn't it about time we became righteous enough through Christ, which will lead to denying self for God's greater glory?

Afterthoughts

I pray that you enjoyed reading about the religious groups that opposed Jesus' teachings the most. But even more so, I pray that you will grasp the principles of Jesus' teachings and the spirit in which the law was given to God's people, and not be bound by it. Moreover, I pray that you begin to teach others the dispensation of the Gospel of Jesus Christ, and not be critical of those that trespass the law of God. I pray that you give to them the discourse of the new covenant, and that God's grace is sufficient enough, along with the help of the Holy Spirit, which will enable them to achieve the moral standards of God's law.

I believe that there exists a degree of Pharisee thinking in all of humankind. In order to guard against this kind of thinking, we must reject the attitudes and behaviors that clearly define a sinful nature. Believers must submit themselves totally unto the Holy Spirit. I realize that it may take some longer than others, before the moral standard of God's law is realized in some people lives. However, achieving the moral standards of the law is the work of the Holy Spirit. You must make a decision to be obedient and put your trust and faith in God. I believe that an impure thought life can lead to negative behavior, thus, impede a believer's spiritual growth.

Therefore, controlling one's thoughts is definitely a measure that can be used to guard against thinking as the Pharisees did. There is a well-known poem attributed to an anonymous author that is worth remembering often by everyone, not only by Christians who want to serve successfully. It reads:

Be careful of your thoughts, for your thoughts become your words.

Be careful of your words, for your words become your actions.

Be careful of your actions, for your actions become your habits.

Be careful of your habits, for your habits become your character.

Be careful of your character, for your character becomes your destiny.

I will conclude by challenging the reader, which the subtitle exalts *"Grow in Grace."* Jesus did.

Section Three

Study Guide

Study Questions

The questions contained within this study guide are designed to assist new converts, during the inception stages of their service to God, and a reminder to the mature believer that salvation is an ongoing process and is nurtured in spiritual growth and development.

What is God's grace?

____
____
____
____
____
____

How does God's grace work?

____
____
____
____
____
____

What does salvation mean?

____
____
____
____
____

How does a believer become saved?

How does God make a believer righteous?

What is the role of the Holy Spirit?

Can you describe the Kingdom of God?

Why is prayer important to a believer?

____

____

____

____

____

Why should you read the Bible?

____

____

____

____

____

What are the fruits of the Spirit?

____

____

____

____

____

What are the fruits of a sinful nature?

____

____

____

____

____

What is a Testimony?

____

____

____

____

____

Why is your testimony important to others?

____

____

____

____

____

____

How should a Christian respond when confronted with conflict?

____

____

____

____

____

What does the word covenant mean?

____

____

____

____

____

What are some of the attributes that are contained within God's new covenant?

____

____

____

____

____

What is sin?

____

____

____

____

____

____

Glossary

<u>Covenant</u>

Covenant is a word that expresses God's gracious purpose toward his people, and also the relationship into which they are thereby brought to Him.

<u>Grace</u>

Grace is a free and underserved love and favor given by God toward man as a sinner.

<u>Holy Spirit</u>

The Holy Spirit is a gift given to believers by God (See Acts Chapter Two).

<u>Kingdom of God</u>

The Kingdom of God is a term that describes the blessedness of the followers of Christ, particularly attained in this life, and perfectly in the world to come.

<u>Prayer</u>

Prayer is an offering to God, petitions for mercies desired, and thanksgiving and praise for blessings received.

<u>Salvation</u>

In the New Testament, salvation is the word used to denote the deliverance from sin and death through faith in Christ.

<u>Sin</u>

Sin is a transgression of the law of God (1John 3:4). All unrighteousness is sin. Sin is lawlessness.

<u>Testimony</u>

A testimony is a solemn affirmation made for the purpose of establishing or providing a true whole revelation of God's will)

Biography

John Clinton's early life presented many trials and obstacles that he had to work to overcome. He was born in Clarksdale, Mississippi, a small rural town approximately sixty miles south of Memphis, Tennessee. His socially and economically depressed neighborhood was a typical haven for drugs, alcohol, and all the illegal activities that went along with abuse of these substances. During his school years, he was considered "at risk" because of poor academic and poor school attendance, which resulted in a series of juvenile court convictions. John's mother died when he was only twelve years old. He and his seven siblings were divided among foster homes and relatives, and some were caught up in the juvenile court system.

During his military service, John learned the value of an education. He holds multiple degrees, an associate in General Studies, a bachelor's in Business Administration from Liberty University, Lynchburg, Virginia, a master's in Theology and a doctorate in Religion from Christian Bible College, Rocky Mount, North Carolina.

John offers his assistance as a spiritual leader by speaking locally at churches, and to groups that support societal needs in general. He also volunteers to serve at food banks, homeless shelters, youth programs, bible studies, and other outreach endeavors, striving to serve in the manner and example of Jesus.

John is also the author of *The Release of God's Provision*, (Dorrance Publishing Company, Pittsburgh, Pennsylvania, 2001, *Bringing in the Sheep, A Guide to Christian Leadership,*

2003, and *Triumphing in Adversity*, PublishAmerica, Frederick, Maryland, 2004). John is also proud to be of service to others in their publishing endeavors, especially his daughter Sherri Cheeks, God Listens Too, PublishAmerica, Fredrick, Maryland.

9 780980 135749